THIS BULLET GRID JOURNAL BELONGS TO:

_____

SOME SIMPLE LAYOUTS
to get you started

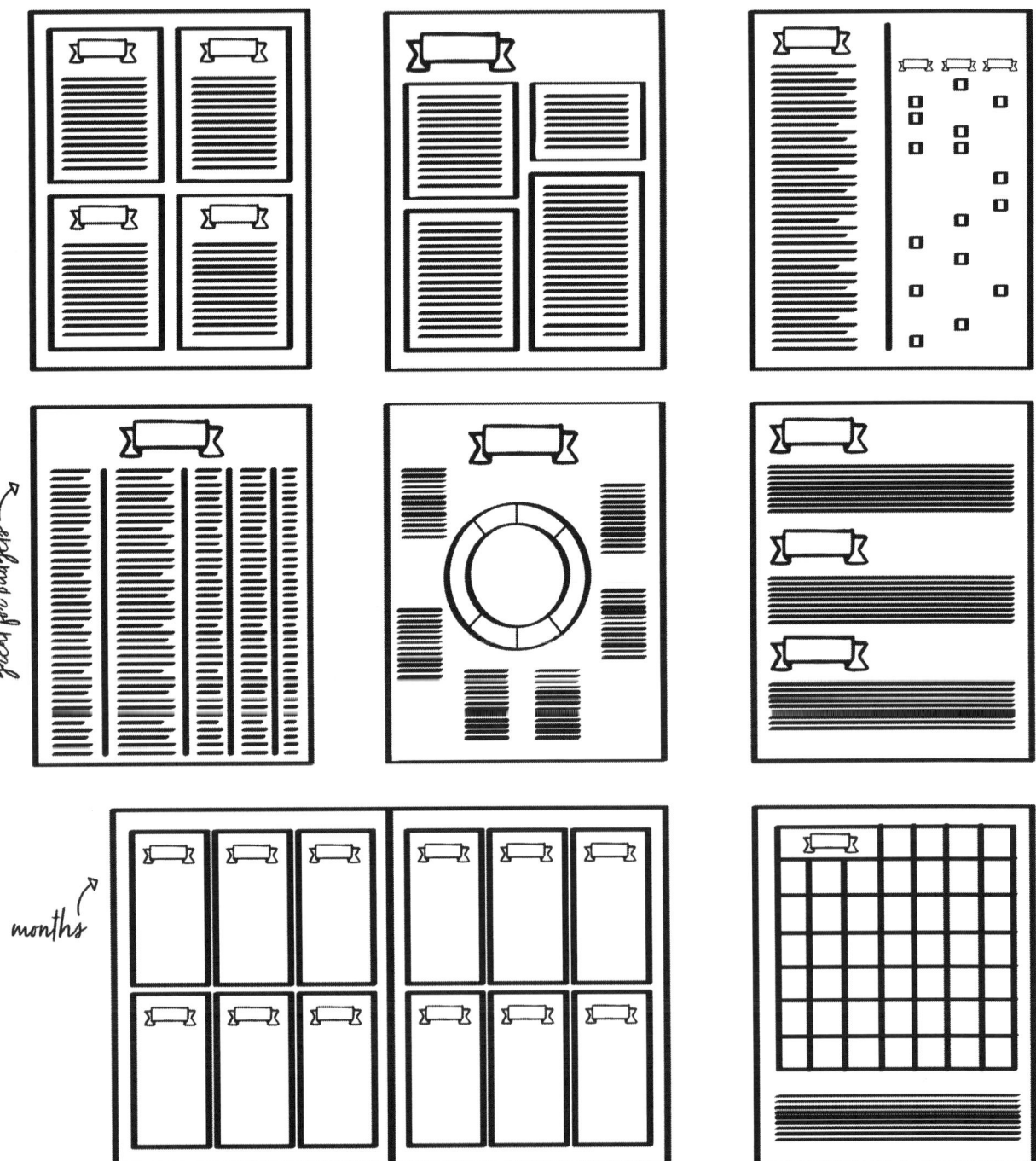

A LITTLE ADDITIONAL *inspiration*

- BUDGETS/FINANCIALS
- GROCERY LISTS
- MEAL PLANNING
- FITNESS LOG
- WEEKLY CHORES
- COURSE PLANNING
- SELF CARE
- APPOINTMENTS
- HOLIDAY SHOPPING LIST
- BOOKS TO READ
- IMPORTANT DATES
- BIRTHDAYS
- SLEEP TRACKING
- WATER TRACKING
- DEADLINES
- RECIPES
- ACCOMPLISHMENTS
- DOODLING
- EXAMS
- GOALS & DREAMS
- CALENDAR
- MEDICINE
- HABIT TRACKING
- DAILY TO-DO LISTS
- DIARY WRITING
- MEMORIES
- STORYWRITING
- BOOKS TO READ
- TRAVEL PLANS
- SONG LISTS
- SCRAPBOOKING
- PARTY PLANNING
- BUCKET LIST
- AND MUCH MORE!

CREATE YOUR
Key

...AND GO!